MANAGING CLASSROOM LEARNING

A Guide for Improving Test Scores

Kenneth M. Matthews

UNIVERSITY
PRESS OF
AMERICA

LANHAM • NEW YORK • LONDON

Copyright © 1984 by Kenneth M. Matthews

University Press of America,™ Inc.

4720 Boston Way
Lanham. MD 20706

3 Henrietta Street
London WC2E 8LU England

Library of Congress Cataloging in Publication Data

Matthews, Kenneth M., 1940–
    Managing classroom learning.

    Includes bibliographical references.
    1. Teaching. 2. Academic achievement. 3. Classroom
management. 4. Interaction analysis in education. I. Title.
LB1025.2.M377 1983   371.1'02   83–19677
ISBN 0–8191–3620–4 (alk. paper)
ISBN 0–8191–3621–2 (pbk. : alk. paper)

All University Press of America books are produced on acid-free
paper which exceeds the minimum standards set by the National
Historical Publications and Records Commission.

PREFACE

Numerous authors have attempted to develop theories to provide direction for educational practice. Yet, the need for conceptual models continues to be great. This need does not exist because previous theories have not been useful. Nor does it indicate practitioners have not attempted to use existing theories to guide their activities. The need continues because existing knowledge of the school-related causes of differences in achievement has not proven to be an adequate foundation for the complex task of improving academic performance.

This publication is a report of the results of years of trying to understand why some students are high achievers while others fail. It is based on scholarly reports of research findings, the publications of eminent theorists, and practical experience. Insight arising from these findings, theories, and experiences have led to the conclusion that high achieving students tend to be taught by teachers who are different in several significant ways.

The theory presented in this book provides a comprehensive and realistic foundation for effective educational practice. It does not consider factors beyond the direct influence of normal schooling processes. Rather, it identifies key variables affected by activities within schools which impact heavily on academic performance. Obviously, as knowledge of human behavior increases, the theory will need to be refined and supplemented. However, it does provide a needed conceptual foundation to guide current educational practice.

The utility of educational theory is limited by the extent it can be applied in field settings. Yet, the antiseptic nature of much theory does not encourage its use in the contaminated environment of schools. Therefore, to facilitate application in field settings, discussion focuses on methods of creating specific, desireable conditions. General strategies for providing appropriate learning experiences, using resources, exerting effective leadership, and developing an internalized locus of control are described. In addition, systematic procedures for developing coordinated plans are presented.

iii

This monograph provides the foundation for comprehensive and realistic approaches to improve student achievement. It contains both elements of successful programs - a sound theoretical base and practical methods. I hope those who are committed to improving academic performance find it useful.

TABLE OF CONTENTS

FIGURES

THEORY*

Educators are faced with increasing demands for greater efficiency in producing better educational products. Many publications have focused on the concepts and technology of measuring efficiency in the delivery of educational products.[1] Other prominent reports have focused attention on the complexities of interactions among societal and schooling variables on educational outcomes.[2] The central challenge is one of finding more efficient ways of utilizing scarce resources to produce better educational outcomes.

Those who attempt to improve the academic performance of students through the application of research findings are soon aware of ambiguity and inconsistency in the literature. The status of educational research is not so precisely refined as to indicate strategies yielding consistent success.[3] The most humbling conclusion may be that no variants of existing educational systems are found to be consistently related to educational outcomes for students.[4] Perhaps the most frustrating possibility is that the same treatment may affect different students in diametrically opposite ways.[5] These conclusions are precisely what might be expected if teaching is recognized as an art and learning as a highly individualized process.

With the information available, educators must choose between no action or action based upon inadequate evidence. The more defensible plans recognize the individualistic nature of the teaching-learning process, take into consideration interactive effects of multiple factors, and focus on those variables educators have some power to influence.[6] In the following pages a conceptual model will be developed which focuses on factors educators can influence and includes consideration of interactive effects of these factors on academic performance.[7]

---

*Adapted from: "Improving Academic Performance," **Educational Forum** Vol. XLIV(November 1979), pp. 59-69. The key elements of the theory were published earlier in "Schooling and Learning - The Principals Influence on Student Achievement," **NASSP Bulletin** Vol. 60, No. 402, (October 1976), pp. 1-15.

1

Ability and Performance

Assumption One - Ability to perform is a function of the interactive effects of experience and inherited potential to benefit from experience.

Ability is a basic correlate of academic achievement in that it is consistently related to school performance.[8] However, ability is the product of interactions between the individual and the environment. Born with varying degrees of potential to profit from experience, individuals develop varying levels of ability to achieve in school.

Serious questions have been raised over the extent innate capacity to learn places practical limits on performance. McClelland and his colleagues concluded that, with moderate levels of intelligence, it is possible to be one of the world's greatest scientists.[9] Brookover and Erickson pointed out that, although genetic differences do exist, they do not make a discernable difference in many cases.[10]

Others have indicated concern for the relative importance of structured experiences on academic performance. Gagne asserted knowledge acquisition is a process in which every new capability is built upon a foundation of previously learned capabilities.[11] Averch suggested that the sequencing and organization of instruction may be even more important than the medium.[12]

While educators cannot alter the inherited potential of students, they do have tremendous influence over the organization of learning experiences. It is axiomatic to say students will have greater ability in trigonometry, physics, or French when they have received instruction in these subjects than when they have had no exposure.[13] If students are expected to have the ability to achieve in specific content areas, they should be provided learning experiences in the same areas. To do otherwise is illogical. Students must receive instruction in the cognitive content areas that tests are designed to measure or lower levels of performance on those tests must be expected.

Assumption Two - Ability to perform is a threshold variable.

2

Although ability to perform is a prerequisite to performance, the relationship between ability and performance is not linear for all tasks. In addition, the threshold level for each task may be unique. For example, if a student has the ability to compute the slope of a given line with integer Cartesian coordinates, then he/she can compute the slope of a line. With increased ability the student can still only compute the slope of a line. Greater ability may enable more efficient performance, but as long as the task remains the same one cannot become more effective at that task. Within this construct, fixed response tasks encouraging convergent thought, such as those included on most tests of academic performance require only a threshold level of ability for effective performance. The challenge is to make certain that students are provided with learning experiences enabling them to have the ability to perform on specific measures of academic performance, and, at the same time, ensure that resources are not allocated toward increasing ability when greater ability is not warranted.

Effort and Performance

Assumption Three - Effort to perform is influenced by self-concept of ability and desire to perform.

Effective performance requires a focus of energy or effort on the task. According to Smith and Cranny, effort or intention are the only variables directly influencing performance.[14] However, specific strategies influencing effort on a consistent manner have remained elusive. In fact, strategies effective for all individuals may not be in the realm of possibility. Averch concluded there is not a "right" way to teach.[15] In spite of this limitation, direction is found in the literature toward general principles which can be applied to specific situations.

Factors effecting motivation have been studied by numerous scholars. One of the more comprehensive investigations of motivation was conducted by Vroom.[16] He explained motivation as a function of the algebraic sum of the product of the individual's perceived probabilities of successes and the desirability of these successes.[17] Atkinson assumed that the performance of the individual is a multiplicative

3

function of the strength of expectancy that performance
will be followed by success, relative attractiveness of
success, and general motivation to succeed.[18] In
studying factors related to academic achievement
Coleman found interest in learning and self-concept to
be among those factors having the strongest
relationships to academic achievement. Self-concept
appeared to be particularly important for students from
advantaged backgrounds.[19]

Self-concept seems to be as closely related to
academic performance as mental ability.[20] However,
Brookover found self-concept of ability to be a more
powerful predictor of achievement than general
self-esteem.[21] According to Shavelson, self-concepts
are related to academic experience.[22] Although academic
self-concept logically follows from academic
experience, Brookover and Erickson reported one study
where changes in self-concepts of ability were followed
by changes in academic achievement.[23] The work of
Atkinson lead him to conclude that manipulation of
strength of expectancy of success is the most feasible
means of changing achievement oriented motivation.[24]

These authors have provided direction for
strategies to influence effort by focusing on
motivation. Strategies to influence effort should be
directed toward students' self-concepts of ability to
succeed academically and desire to achieve in school.

Nonlinear Relationships

**Assumption Four - Relationships between factors
affecting effort and performance are not linear.**

The influence of motivational factors on effort
and the effect of effort on performance are not simple.
Atkinson pointed out that motivational conditions
producing inhibition and a decrement in performance may
be greatest when the perceived probability of success
is intermediate.[25] However, he also indicated
inhibition may enhance performance when an individual
is too highly motivated.[26] Highly motivated individuals
seem to perform more efficiently when the perceived
probability of success is only moderately high.
Increases in motivation, up to some optimal point,
appear to increase efficiency. Beyond that point,
increases in motivation tend to lead to a decrease in

efficiency.[27] More positive self-concepts of ability, up to some point, may contribute to increased effort. Beyond that point, more positive self-concepts may lead to debilitating procrastination of effort.

Moderately high levels of desire and moderately positive self-concepts of ability appear to be conditions most conducive to efficient and productive effort. Plans to improve academic performance should be designed to ensure that minimal levels of effort are being exerted, but students are not so highly motivated that dysfunctional levels of anxiety contribute to less productive effort. Strategies should be implemented to foster positive self-concepts of ability, but not to the extent that the result is procrastination.

Resources and Performance

Assumption Five - External resources facilitate performance.

The extent human and material resources enable students to achieve more efficiently and effectively has not been clearly demonstrated. Averch concluded that school resources, at best, contribute one to five percent in the prediction of achievement.[28] Weiss offered one explanation for the small differences attributed to school variables. He asserted that most American schools are far more alike than different and, within the existing normative range, the variations which do exist simply do not produce dramatic differences in student learning.[29] One source claims school resources do make a difference, provided they are properly allocated and targeted. Apparently many research studies have assumed consistent benefits for all students when differential effects are a more logical explanation.[30] Brown found only one of thirteen school-related variables to be an efficient predictor of student achievement among schools in a statewide study. This variable was expenditure per student for instruction. He concluded instructional expenditures had differential effects in that increased availability of better quality instructional resources would benefit low achieving school populations more than those with high achievement.[31]

Because the nature of the influence of external resources on academic performance has not been clearly demonstrated, the use of individual judgment appears to be the best direction indicated. The relationship between external resources and academic performance may be such that the contributions of external resources to academic performance differ among students with different learning styles, as well as among the various curricular content areas.

Leadership Influence

Assumption Six - Leadership influences desire to perform.

Leadership is considered to be the act of guiding the efforts of organizational subordinates toward organizational objectives. Although leadership is an art, it can be improved through an understanding and application of science. Information provided by behavioral scientists is useful in leadership attempts to influence efforts through the variable factor of desire to perform.

Of the three types of influence described by Etzioni,[34] Lipham and Hoeh considered only normative power remaining in principal-teacher relations.[35] Although coercive and renumerative power may be available to teachers in their leadership of students, they are not frequently associated with the potent influences of moral commitment. Of nine possible power-involvement relations, moral involvement is more commonly associated with normative power.[36]

Additional leadership considerations have been investigated by others. Under a theory Y style of leadership, as described by McGregor, an organizational climate whereby individual goals can best be met by efforts towards organizational goals is considered most productive.[37] The classic model of Getzels and Guba also stresses integration of individual need-dispositions and institutional-expectations.[38] The managerial grid of Blake and Mouton indicates organizations will be most effective when concern is expressed for both the individual and for production.[39] Hertzberg concluded subordinates will be motivated when they have opportunities to demonstrate capabilities.[40] Fiedler's contingency theory assumes leadership style and favorableness of situation are important determinants of leadership effectiveness.[41]

Strategies facilitating effective leadership have not been clearly defined. However, the writings of the better known theorists provide direction. Prominent theorists suggest a focus on performance and a focus on individuality in human relations as important considerations for effective leaders. In addition to an emphasis on production and human relations, one other consideration underlies much of the leadership theory. This consideration is ethics. Ethical practice has been considered an essential element of acceptable leadership for many years.[42]

Assumption Seven - Attitudes toward the superior, perceptions of superior's value on performance, and perceived future utility of performance influence the desire of subordinates to perform.

Attitudes appear to be highly significant factors in human behavior.[43] Likert concluded changes in attitudes generally precede changes in productive behavior in organizations.[44] Although the social backgrounds of students appear to be dominant factors in their attitudes and patterns of behavior,[45] these may be modified through social interaction within the schools.[46] McDill et al. found evidence to support their position that academic behavior was affected by differences in social and educational environments among schools. They indicated the greater the intrinsic value of knowledge supported by the school environment and the stronger the emotional support given to students by teachers, the more likely students are to achieve high test scores.[47]

Although inconsistency will be observed if attention is directed only at the attitudes of subordinates toward superiors, the predispositions of subordinates to respond to leadership acts are affected by their attitudes toward the leader.[48] The more one likes another, the more justification one has for performing even disagreeable acts for a "friend."[49] Friendship may be considered only one type of attitude. "Acceptance of the organizational superior" may be a more appropriate description of critical relationships between attitudes toward superiors and the behavior of subordinates. Fiedler considered subordinates' attitudes toward the leader to affect their behavior when they accepted the leader.[50]

7

The direction of subordinates' response predispositions is influenced by their preceptions of the direction of the superior's leadership. If perceived as leading toward improved academic performance, then subordinates' positive attitudes toward the superior will have a positive effect on their desire to improve academic performance.

Averch contended teachers' expectations probably influence student behavior and perhaps academic achievement.[51] Brookover and Erickson reported a similar position. In fact, they asserted that nearly all students meet the minimum knowledge and skill levels expected by the school staff.[52] Although not clearly documented, the influence of the expectations of teachers on students' academic achievement does have support in the literature.[53]

Perception of the future utility of performance affects performance. Individuals tend to attach more importance to those aspects of organizational roles they perceive as contributing to their welfare. Though the overall effect of teachers on students' perceptions of the utility of schooling may be small in relation to the experiences associated with the socioeconomic backgrounds of students, this factor is one where teachers do have the potential to influence the motivation of students. According to Atkinson, the motivational implications of students seeing a contingent relationship between success in school and attainment of long-term goals is particularly important because it is teachable.[54] McDill has provided some evidence that educational climates can be established in which schooling is valued beyond that predicted from the backgrounds of students.[55]

The attitudes of students toward teachers, students' perceptions of teachers' values on academic performance, and students' perceptions of the future utility of success in school are useful and ethical considerations in developing plans for improving academic performance.

Interactive Effects

Assumption Eight - There are interactive effects among factors affecting academic performance.

Ability, effort, and external resources may each have a unique influence on academic performance. However, the interactive effects are more critical than the simple effects of the three factors. For example, if an individual has the threshold level of ability and adequate resources to accomplish the task, but does not exert sufficient effort, then effective performance will not occur. But effort alone will not be productive unless ability and adequate resources exist. One possible explanation of relations among these variables and academic performance is that academic performance (P) is a function (f) of the interactive effects of ability (A), external resources (R), and effort (E). In symbolic form, these relations may be expressed as: $P = f(A \times R \times E)$.

When the effects of those factors influencing ability and effort are taken into consideration, the preceding symbolic expression becomes more complex. Ability is assumed to be affected by inherited capacity to learn (I) and learning experiences (L). By substitution, the expession now becomes: $P = f(I \times L \times R \times E)$. Effort, in turn, is influenced by two variables, desire (D) and self-concept of ability (C). Desire to achieve is affected by numerous factors. However, at least three can be influenced by in-school experiences. Experiences in school affect students' attitudes toward teachers (T), perceptions of teachers' values (V), and perceptions of the future utility of school (U). Thus, the influence of school experiences on academic performance (Ps) may be expressed as a function of six identifiable variables.[56] Primary relations among these variables are demonstrated in the figure, "Schooling and Academic Performance." In symbolic form, the hypothetical effect of schooling on academic performance is: $Ps = f(L \times R \times T \times V \times U \times C)$.

As Figure 1 illustrates, simplistic strategies that focus on only one or two of the six factors are not likely to consistently result in higher academic improvement. A comprehensive plan to influence all six factors, as well as to produce desirable interactions,

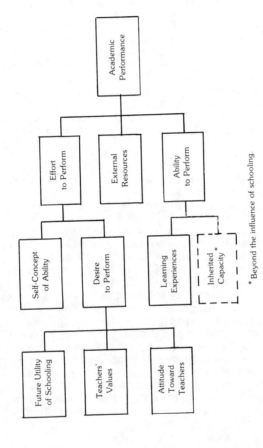

Figure 1 - Schooling and Academic Performance[57]

* Beyond the influence of schooling.

10

would appear to be a more logical approach to improving academic performance.

Differential Effects

Assumption Nine - Specific acts may have differing effects on factors affecting academic performance.

An act which has a positive influence on one of the six schooling factors affecting academic performance may have negative effects on others. The possibilities for differing effects among these factors and on the numerous interactive combinations of the six factors make predictions of success for specific acts difficult, if not impossible. However, predictions of effects on pairs of the six factors can be made.

Of the fifteen possible pairs of the six factors, the potential for differing effects on members of two pairs warrant close scrutiny. These pairs are: (1) students' perceptions of the future utility of schooling and learning experiences, and (2) students' self-concepts of ability and perceptions of the value teachers place on academic performance.

A strategy which may be proposed to improve students' perceptions of the future utility of schooling is to focus classroom activities on those aspects of the curriculum which students perceive as being pragmatic. This strategy may result in increased effort to achieve in school. But, if the content measured is not taught, then a high level of performance is not a likely outcome. On the other hand, if strict adherence is made to teaching the skills and concepts measured by norm referenced tests, then students may perceive the content to have little utility. The implications of this possibility are serious. In some situations educators may face a seemingly unresolvable dilemna--to attempt to teach content students perceive as impractical or to measure performance on content not taught.

A strategy commonly used to create positive self-concepts of ability is to make high grades easy to obtain with little effort. This same strategy may result in students perceiving their teachers as valuing academic performance little and having low expectations. If expectations are set at such a high

11

level students believe the standards to be totally unreasonable, then students may believe they have little or no hope of meeting teacher expectations.

Implications of the Theory

The complexities of interactive effects among factors affecting academic performance and differential effects of specific acts on factors affecting academic performance offer little hope of specific variants of schooling yielding consistent results. If teaching is accepted as an art and learning as a highly individualized process, then theoretical foundations are the best tools available to educators for the improvement of academic performance.

STRUCTURING EXPERIENCES*

There is little doubt that both a threshold level of potential to benefit from experience and experience itself are necessary in order for academic accomplishments to occur. The debate that exists in this area centers on the relative importance of the inherited capacity to learn and the contributions of learning experiences to academic performance. However, from the perspective of the educational practitioner, the primary concerns are for the limitations imposed by the genetically determined potentials of individual students and the identification of logical structures for the experiences to be provided to students.

Genetic Limitations

Although the precise nature of the functioning of the human brain is not clearly understood, certain premises are generally accepted. Within the range of human intellectual potentials are found individuals whose functional activities indicate only rudimentary thought processes, as well as those who demonstrate superior speed and capabilities in assimilating and processing information. Anyone who has visited resident institutions for the mentally retarded would find it difficult to ignore the very strong evidence that severe limitations on intellectual potential can be imposed by genetic inadequacies. At the other extreme are those who exhibit the capacity to master extremely complex concepts with great speed and little apparent effort.

The evidence clearly indicates strong support for the premise that the ability to profit from schooling experiences is affected by inherited capacity to learn from experience. The implications for teaching methodologies are apparent. Some students will not master concepts as rapidly as others. Even though

---

*Portions of this chapter were taken from: Kenneth M. Matthews and C. Thomas Holmes, "Improving Test Scores -- How to Develop Comprehensive Plans," **The NASSP Bulletin**, Vol. 67 No. 460, (February 1983), pp. 104-112.

teaching may not always be individualized, the rate at which learning occurs is always individual specific. The key to selecting appropriate teaching strategies lies in the identification of the optimal pace at which individuals are able to profit from the experience.

Simply because some individuals do not learn as rapidly as others is an inadequate basis to support a belief that many students cannot master the skills and concepts taught in elementary and secondary schools. Upon serious reflection, most individuals would find it difficult to identify any specific course where the content was beyond their intellectual capacity to learn once the "language" of the course was mastered. Much of the difficulty students attribute to particular courses encountered in the schooling process can be directly linked to factors other then limitations imposed by intellectual capacity.

Knowledge of the terms used is the foundation for learning in many of the courses commonly considered conceptually difficult. The most obvious examples are the foreign languages. Without knowledge of the vocabulary and grammatical principles success in foreign language courses is not likely. However, the learning of specific vocabulary words and grammatical principles can be as elementary as simple memorization which is not unduly taxing for the average intellect. In fact, the overwhelming majority of the people to whom a language is native rather than foreign learn the language. To assume that German is conceptually too difficult for most Americans to learn is absurd. Granted, most Americans would find the German language more difficult than Germans. This is because Americans are not provided with the wealth of German learning experiences that are available to the natives of Germany.

Vocabulary mastery is easily recognized as necessary for acceptable levels of achievement in foreign languages. However, similar conditions exist for most courses of study, even in such areas as advanced mathematics and statistics. For example, knowledge of the meaning of certain mathematical terms is necessary before students can reasonably be expected to successfully solve the following equation:

$$X = (Sin\ A - Tan\ B)^{-3}$$

Obviously, more than a knowledge of the meanings of Sin and Tan are required for solution of the equation. But, the intellectual processes involved in finding the value of X are comparable to those involved in the subtraction of fractions with different denominators such as:

$$2/3 - 5/16$$

Yet, most people assume that many students do not have the intellectual capacity to learn to solve trigonometry problems and that almost all students can learn to subtract fractions.

Although some academic skills and concepts require higher levels of inherited capacity to learn than others, the limitations imposed by genetics on academic performance tend to be grossly exaggerated. The point here is that genetic limitations severely limit the learning potential of only exceptional students.

Logical Structures

There are no firm data indicating a clearly superior organization of learning experiences for improving academic performance. The simple fact is that there are alternative ways of reaching the same academic goals. Perhaps the most important consideration in structuring learning experiences is making certain that the skills and concepts to be measured are taught. The logical first step in this process is identifying the skills and concepts to be measured.

Regardless of the type of measuring tool to be used, no serious attempt to improve academic performance can afford to ignore the necessity of making a determination of the skills and concepts to be assessed. Criterion-referenced examinations may make the process less arduous than norm-referenced tests, but the process is essentially the same. Objectives can be established and then assessment procedures established or assessment procedures can be determined first and then instructional objectives formulated. In other words, we can test what we teach or we can teach what we test. The alternatives to these procedures are undesirable if improvement on specific measures of academic performance is the goal.

Diagnosis

Once the measurement instrument has been determined the task of diagnosing group and individual needs becomes the logical second step in structuring experiences to improve the ability of students. Just as the limitations imposed by inherited potentials to benefit from learning experiences are often grossly over-estimated, the advantages of building learning foundations are commonly given inadequate consideration. For example, suppose students were asked to tell if the following statement is true or false:

"Of moment, mastery learning obtains in spite of the inveterate misanthropic."

Without knowledge of secondary meanings of "moment" and "obtains" as well as an understanding of the words "inveterate" and "misanthropic" there is little likelihood students will be able to give a rational response to the item. Without this foundational information the logic of the statement would be immaterial. Cognitive processing strategies are dependent upon the mental interpretation of the bits of information to be processed. Worth noting at this point is that simply improving one's vocabulary may be inadequate unless the words "moment", "obtains", "inveterate", and "misanthropic" are included in the expanded vocabulary.

The specific bits of information to be processed cannot be discerned independent of an analysis of the body of knowledge included on the assessment instrument. This means the measuring tool should be analyzed thoroughly, not only in terms of the cognitive areas included, but also in terms of the information presented for processing. Until this process is completed learning need-assessments have little meaning.

Assuming the measurement tool has been selected and analyzed, then diagnosis of individual needs can be made. The most effective diagnosis can probably be made by using the identical instrument for both diagnostic and evaluative purposes. Barring this as a viable option, the content included on the post-test should be presented in a parallel form on the diagnostic tool.

16

Analysis of the results of the administration of the diagnostic tool will yield data relative to the specific questions answered correctly as well as those answered incorrectly by both individuals and by the group as a whole. When any question has been answered correctly by the vast majority of the group it would generally be safe to assume the group would not benefit substantially by further instruction in that particular content. However, this does not mean significant benefits would not accrue to individuals who missed the test item. In other words, although the diagnostic process for groups and individuals would be essentially the same, the results may be distinctly different. Measurement error makes diagnosis of individual needs more difficult than for groups. Individuals may be considered initially in need of instructional assistance for all test items missed.

Test items missed by most members of the group or items missed by individuals can be subjected to a second level of diagnosis once they have been identified. At this level a determination can be made as to whether the items answered incorrectly were missed because the necessary skills and concepts were not mastered or because students were unable to comprehend the information to be processed or both.

Although several strategies may be developed to determine reasons why students missed specific test items, two relatively simple techniques will generally prove to be adequate. (Assuming, of course, that students seriously attempted to answer the questions). The first technique is that of asking students to explain what the missed test item asked them to do. The second technique is to present the same task using a different format and different words and then asking the students to answer the question. The first technique will identify those students who are unable to comprehend the question asked. The second will identify those who lack mastery of the skills and concepts necessary to give accurate responses. When completed, these tasks provide critical information for the creation of instructional strategies to provide appropriate learning experiences.

Prescription

The diagnostic procedures described above will provide the basic data to begin the task of providing the structure for appropriate learning experiences. Specific test items missed and the probable reasons students did not give correct responses will have been identified. These data place students into three categories for each test item missed; (1) those who do not understand the question, (2) those who cannot answer the question because of inadequate cognitive skill, and (3) those who neither comprehend the question nor have adequate skill to give accurate responses even if they understand the question.

Of the three groups of students identified above the most dramatic progress can be accomplished by working with those students who do not understand the questions, but can give accurate responses when the problem is restated in different terms. For these students improvement in academic performance can be accomplished rather easily. Simply providing them with the information which will enable them to decode the message will give them the ability to answer the question. The other two groups pose more difficult problems.

When students understand the problem, but are unable to solve it the instructional task becomes one of determining an appropriate sequence of experiences leading to competency. As teachers know, there is not a unique sequence of experiences which will prove to be effective for all students. The key is in selecting a sequence that is effective for most students and providing alternatives for the other students.

There is no magic in determining an appropriate sequence of learning experiences. Examination of the sequential processes used by most competent individuals will generally yield an appropriate sequence. For example, consider the following problem:

$$X = 2/3 - 5/16$$

One sequence which is used successfully is:

1st - Finding a common denominator.

$$3 \times 16 = 48$$

18

        2nd - Creating a new expression for
              each fraction using the common
              denominator.

              48/3 = 16,   16 x 2 = 32,   32/48

              48/16 = 3,   3 x 5 = 15,   15/48

    3rd - Subtracting numerators.

              32/48 - 15/48 = 17/48

Upon close inspection it becomes apparent that mastery
of the skills involved in multiplication, subtraction,
and division of whole numbers should occur before
attempting to teach subtraction of fractions with
different denominators. Given this information there
are five distinct skills involved in solving problems
of subtracting fractions with unlike denominators;

    (A) Multiplying, Subtracting, and Dividing Whole
        Numbers

    (B) Finding Common Denominators

    (C) Computing Equivalent Fractions Given New
        Denominators

    (D) Subtracting Fractions with Common
        Denominators

    (E) Reducing Fractions

    One logical sequence for teaching these skills
would be A, E, C, B, and then D. Although A, C, D, E,
and then B would be an alternative sequence, each of
the five skills should be mastered before students can
reasonably be expected to subtract fractions with
different denominators. Teachers of mathematics would
find little difficulty in teaching each of the five
skills to students with normal potential provided they
are given adequate time. The individual skills are
simply not that difficult. The major problem lies in
the volume of bits of information to be learned and in
development of the cognitive strategies for processing
the information.

19

The third group of students, those who do not understand the problem and could not solve it if they did, constitute the most difficult of the three instructional groups. These students must not only master the information to be processed, but also the cognitive strategies involved in processing the information. However, over time, almost all students can be taught the prerequisite information and cognitive strategies.

Information Mastery

Regardless of the volume of information to be mastered the individual pieces are learned one at a time. In structuring learning experiences for information mastery the essential first step is to identify the specific bits of information to be learned. Whether the area of information mastery is mathematics, science, social studies, language arts, or industrial arts the process is the same. One cannot teach vocabulary. One can only teach specific words. Science cannot be taught. Only specific scientific data, skills, and concepts can be taught. A body of knowledge is not mastered as a whole. It is learned one piece at a time.

In the process of choosing the assessment tool to be used the skills and concepts to be measured are determined. The items on the selected instrument provide the data necessary for identification of the information to be mastered. If mathematical questions ask students to compute the area of a rectangle, then they should be taught that the area of a rectangle is equal to the product of the length times the height. If the vocabulary words are selected from the Dolch Basic Reading Vocabulary list, then students should be taught these words. If the social studies questions require knowledge of the issues involved in Civil War, then they should be taught these issues. In other words, the information to be taught is dependent upon the information to be processed in responding to the academic performance measure.

For many educators the process of identifying the information to be mastered will be a traumatic experience. Many will find it extremely difficult to become precise in their information mastery expectations. Others will question the ethics of the activity. These feelings are understandable and the ethics may be debated. No reputable educator would advocate teaching only the specific content measured. However, test items are generally considered indicative of rather specific content areas. No reasonable teacher would teach that 7 x 3 = 21 only because this item was on the test when it is obvious the question was selected to assess knowledge of multiplication facts.

Regardless of the measurement tool selected, students must be taught the information to be processed in order to respond to the test items or low levels of academic performance of that instrument should be expected. Once students have the basic information required for processing, then the far more difficult problem of developing cognitive strategies can be attacked.

Cognitive Strategies

Any description of appropriate procedures for developing effective cognitive strategies must at this point in time be highly speculative. The scientific basis for learning simply has not developed to the point that we can reliably predict how individuals **will think**. What can be done, however, is to describe a process by which students **can think** and use that as the beginning point to plan for the development of effective cognitive strategies.

Cognitive strategies for processing information for the resolution of problems range from the very simple to extremely complex. Some test items require only a recall response to a stimulus which has been presented in the test item. Others require the recall of information and an appropriate ordering of cognitive processes. Choosing the correct meaning from four or five alternatives for the word "invigilate" can be classified as simple recall. Finding the correct answer to a verbal problem requiring the solution of simultaneous algebraic equations is far more complex.

As long as the measuring tool is designed to stimulate convergent rather than divergent thought the instructional task can be one of providing students with models of cognitive strategies which can be employed and giving them experience in applying these

21

strategies. An example of cognitive processing at an intermediate level of difficulty illustrates how students can be taught cognitive processing strategies.

Suppose students were presented with the following problem:

"Two cars traveling in the same direction on an interstate highway passed Exit 21 at 10:00 a.m. Car A was moving at 75 miles an hour and Car B was moving at 50 miles an hour. At 11:00 a.m. Car A was stopped by the highway patrol for speeding. Just as Car A was pulling back on the highway Car B passed by. If both cars traveled at constant speeds what time was it when Car B passed Car A?"

In processing this information several steps are involved. One sequence which can be employed is:

1st - Where was Car A at 11:00 a.m.

1 hour x 75 mph = 75 miles from Exit 21?

2nd - How long would it take Car B to travel 75 miles?

75 miles divided by 50 mph = 1 and 1/2 hours

3rd - What time is it 1 and 1/2 hours after 10:00 a.m.?

10:00 plus 1 and 1/2 hours = 11:30 a.m.

Although other cognitive strategies may be employed to solve the preceding problem, the model strategy presented will suffice for dealing with all problems of the same type. Instructional techniques for teaching students to apply this cognitive strategy would appropriately involve two steps. Step one would be to illustrate the cognitive processing strategy and step two would be for students to practice using the strategy on problems of the same type. With repetition, nearly all students will master the techniques involved in applying the model cognitive strategy.

Model strategies for the processing of information can be developed for all types of problems represented on tests of academic ability and students can be provided with opportunities to experience success in applying these cognitive strategies. Through these experiences students can learn to select and apply appropriate strategies to those exercises requiring the processing of information.

USING RESOURCES

Although the precise nature of the contributions of external resources to academic performance has not been clearly demonstrated, there is little doubt human and material resources enhance learning. An understanding of the potential benefits of using external resources offers a sound basis for the selection and effective use of resources.

Potential Contributions

If one assumes that ability and effort are the primary factors affecting performance, then the contribution of external resources is to make given levels of ability and effort more productive. As facilitators of academic performance, external resources can enable individuals to make more efficient use of their efforts or make more effective use of their ability. Some teaching or learning aids allow students to learn with less effort. Others help students learn more than their ability would otherwise permit.

Efficiency in learning is a critical factor in plans to improve academic performance. If achievement is to be maximized the time available must be used efficiently. Time wasted is time that cannot be used to learn new skills and concepts.

Some skills and concepts are difficult, if not impossible, to master without adequate human and material resources. To attempt to teach reading without appropriate materials is ridiculous. To expect teachers to effectively teach most academic content without textbooks or other printed material is irresponsible. Learning in complete isolation from others for extended periods of time is intolerable for normal individuals. In fact, if specialized human and material resources were not available to students in school, then there would be no reason to have schools. Through careful planning and close supervision the use of material and human resources can significantly enhance academic performance.

Selecting Material Resources

Material resources will make the greatest contribution to academic performance when their content focuses directly on the content to be measured. Simply having more library books is not likely to have a significant impact on academic performance. Reading **Gone With the Wind** is not likely to have any positive effect on mathematics test scores. Perhaps, it might facilitate higher scores on social studies examinations, but not if the tests cover only the Renaissance period. Printed materials must closely parallel the content to be measured if they are to have a consistently positive effect on academic performance scores.

Textbooks are the dominant material resource used for instruction. In general, teachers rely on textbooks more than any other printed materials and students are expected to spend more time in school reading textbooks than any other materials. If the content of the textbooks reinforce, supplement, or focus directly on the skills and concepts to be measured they can enhance academic performance. If not, they may enhance learning, but will have no significant impact on achievement test scores.

There is a tendency for many educators to assume a high correlation between the contents of textbooks and the skills and concepts measured by standardized tests. This may or may not be true depending on the specific textbooks and the specific tests. The closer one comes to congruency between the content covered by selected textbooks and the content to be measured, the greater the contribution textbooks can make to improve test scores. Content analysis is the **only** way to determine the extent textbooks cover the same content as measures of academic performance.

Content analysis appropriately begins with the instrument to be used to measure academic performance. The content of each textbook considered for use should be compared with the content to be measured. Those having little content in common with the measuring instrument should be withdrawn from consideration. The remaining textbooks can then be judged as to their probable facilitative contributions. For example, if two textbooks are equal in terms of the extent they cover the same content that is to be measured, then they can be evaluated for such factors as level of reading difficulty and appropriateness of the sequence in which concepts are presented.

The easier a textbook is to read the less assistance students will need in studying the material and the more time will be available to teachers for other instructional activities. In addition, books that are easy to read enable students to learn more academic content with less effort. If competing textbooks are equal in other aspects, then the one that is easiest to read will likely be the most valuable.

The appropriate sequencing of concepts is critical. All publishers assume their textbooks have a logial sequence of content. This is very likely true. However, the sequences presented in textbooks may be very different from the ones preferred and used by teachers within a given school. Unless teachers adjust their instructional activities to be more consistent with the textual sequence, the discrepancies may be dysfunctional. (Many students will have difficulty assimilating dissimilar sequences). It is desirable that the sequence in which information is presented to students by both teacher and textbook be consistent and the books requiring the least adjustment on the part of teachers are preferable.

Other material resources can also facilitate higher academic performance. Workbooks, library books, films, filmstrips, slides, tapes, records, physical models, etc., are valuable material resources. As with textbooks, their potential value will be determined primarily by the extent they focus on the same content as that to be measured. Beyond that, visual, tactile, and auditory aids also have the capacity to make learning more efficient.

Less energy is required to learn some concepts using material resources than is required if students have to develop the concepts without the use of the resources. For example, a motion picture showing the movement of ameoba is a more efficient means of illustrating the flow of protoplasm than having each student prepare a slide and view the process under the microscope. Having no visual aids at all would make the learning process even less efficient. In like manner, a physical model of the four-cycle internal combustion engine can illustrate the processes involved

27

in each of the four strokes more effectively than attempting to develop the same concepts using only chalk and chalkboard.

Material resources can be valuable instructional aids provided they focus on the concepts and skills to be measured. However, human resources may be even more valuable.

Using Human Resources

Human resources have a distinct advantage over material resources. Communication among people can be far more complete than that between an individual and an object, such as a textbook. Communication by means of a physical object is necessarily one-way. Printed materials cannot adjust to feedback from the student. The same may be said for all material resources. Communication among people can be extremely flexible and adaptive.

Efforts to improve academic performance which severely restrict interaction among students will have limited success in the long run. Only uncommonly highly motivated and/or abnormal individuals voluntarily limit interaction with others for extended periods of time in favor of academic pursuits in solitude. To ignore this behavioral characteristic is inadviseable. A more desirable approach is to develop strategies to capitalize on the socialization tendency of mankind rather than to attempt to dramatically alter human nature.

For social interaction to directly facilitate high levels of academic performance the focus of the interaction must be on the skills and concepts to be measured. This is no small task, but significant benefits will accrue to those who are able to direct social activity toward academic goals.

There are several means by which interaction among students and between students and teachers can be used to facilitate higher levels of academic performance. Each has weaknesses as well as strengths. Direct instruction by teachers is generally effective for those who need and are ready to learn the concepts presented by the teacher. However, it is impossible for teachers to personally instruct all students all of

28

the time at the levels at which individuals are working when teachers are responsible for teaching large groups of students. Teacher-aides are useful, but expensive. Probably the most potentially useful, but under-utilized, of human resources are students.

Social groups of students that have formed naturally can be a valuable instructional resource. Students who have formed social groups tend to have developed differentiated roles within those groups. When these groups are kept intact the previously differentiated roles will permit transition from other social activities to academic pursuits within a minimum of adjustment problems. However, when the normative behavior of these social groups is contrary to productive learning activities they should be dissolved.

Simply assigning academic activities to a group of students will not necesarrily result in better performance. Execution of specific activities is always by individuals. Although projects may be productively undertaken by groups, individual components must become the responsibility of someone or they are the responsibility of no one. Once an individual accepts responsibility for a specific component of a learning activity on behalf of his social group peer pressure to follow through becomes a significant motivational force.

Of course, some instructional activities do not readily lend themselves to group processes, but do require interaction. In these instances individual students may require instructional assistance for varying periods of time. Under most circumstances assistance of this kind is provided by the teacher. However, this means that students must frequently wait on the teacher because the teacher is busy helping someone else. Unless these students are permitted to seek assistance from others much valuable time will be wasted.

Student tutorial programs have been used with varying degrees of success. They key element in those programs which have been successful is that the tutor had the necessary knowledge or skill and the student needing assistance was willing to accept the tutor's help. Normally, if teachers establish an academically oriented classroom climate and permit students to ask others for help both elements of the successful tutorial programs will be in effect. Students who sincerely want help will not repeatedly ask someone for assistance who does not have the desired skill or knowledge. Permitting students to select the individual they ask for help also increases the likelihood they will be willing to accept that person's assistance.

EFFECTIVE LEADERSHIP

The motivations of students to achieve in school are strongly influenced by their socialization experiences. Experiences in the home establish the initial, and probably the most enduring, orientations of children toward learning. The importance parents and siblings place on learning is demonstrated to the young child in the daily activities of the family. If family members are seekers of knowledge children tend to believe learning is important. If the family members pursue discretionary activities which are not information-seeking in nature children tend to view learning as less important than alternative forms of activity.

As children enter into social relationships outside the home their orientations toward learning and schooling are modified. They become aware of the value people outside of the family unit place on learning and schooling. Gradually, the values of social peers generally become more influential than those of the family. By adolescence, the importance friends place on schooling critically affects the motivations of students to achieve in school. The strong influence of family and peers may never be overcome by educators. However, teachers can have a positive effect on the motivations of students to achieve in school when they have positive relationships with their students.

Contributions of Human Relations

The human relations skills of teachers are critical to the success they will have in motivating students. Teachers who are disliked by their students must rely primarily on other social influences to motivate their students. A teacher can be hated by students and still get a great deal of effort out of students only if students are already highly motivated to do what their teachers are attempting to teach. Obviously other factors affect student motivation, but teachers who do not have positive relationships with their students cannot have as positive an influence on motivation as those whose students have positive attitudes toward them.

Teachers who are liked by their students have strong potential for motivating students to try harder

31

to achieve in their class. People will do things for their friends that are even contrary to what they feel they "ought" to do. In other words, people will do things they believe are "wrong" for the "right" people. The influence of those who are "significant others" is profound, sometimes frightening. The fact that some individuals have had such a powerful influence that their followers have killed or willingly given their lives for their leaders is well-known. Although strategies which have been used by some leaders to influence others are immoral, unethical, or other-wise unacceptable; other effective strategies are moral, ethical, and justifiably in terms of means and ends.

Personal Interactions

In **The Human Group**, Homans provided a critical analysis of the effects of interactions on the development of sentiments between individuals. The more frequently people interact the stronger their feelings toward each other tend to become. The more people like each other the more they tend to seek frequent interaction. The more people interact the more likely they are to accept the activities of others as legitimate and desireable. As Figure 2 illustrates; attitudes, interactions, and common activities are interrelated. An increase in one tends to result in an increase in the others. Similarly, a decrease in one variable tends to result in a decrease in the other two variables.

Even though more frequent interactions tend to result in more positive attitudes, certain kinds of interactions are more effective than others. Interactions which are competitive, degrading, or non-supportive in nature will contribute little to the development of more positive attitudes. The most effective means of developing positive human relations are to have frequent interactions which result in the participants feeling good about themselves and, consequently, toward those who made them feel good.

Likeable People

To become a significant influence on the lives of students for the benefit of students is a desirable and worthy goal in and of itself. However, for the

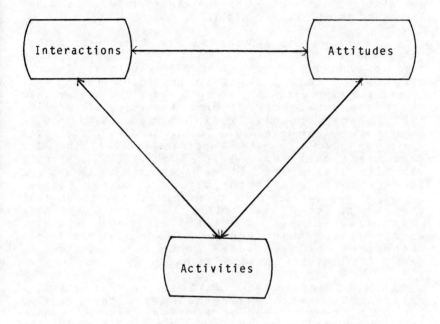

Figure 2 - Interactions and Attitudes

33

purposes of the discussion here, positive relationships with students should be viewed as a means by which teachers can increase the likelihood students will work harder to reach higher levels of academic performance. Although there are no specific behaviors that consistently result in more positive attitudes, there are distinct differences in the kinds of people who are liked and those who are disliked.

People who are cheerful are liked better than those who are "damned ole grouches." Cheerful people tend to evoke positive responses from others. Grouchy people tend to get negative responses from others. People who have even temperaments are liked better than those who are unpredictable. Unpredictable people, particularly organizational superiors, tend to make subordinates feel insecure. People tend to prefer even those who have disagreeable personalities if they are consistent over those who are unpredictable. People who like others are better liked than those who are self-centered and inconsiderate of other people. Self-centered people tend to give the impression that they think they are better than others and most individuals simply do not believe anyone is a more worthy person than they are. Having too positive a concept of one's personal worth is a detriment to developing positive human relations.

Some teachers are able to develop positive relationships with their students rather easily. Others must work hard at getting students to have positive attitudes toward them. However, teachers can choose to behave in ways that indicate to students that they are likeable people.

Teachers can act as if they were cheerful. They can smile, whistle, and laugh. They can avoid being grouchy. Teachers can refrain from complaining. They can be consistent in their interactions with students. Teachers can avoid changing rules indiscriminately. They can behave in ways that indicate they care about students as individuals. Teachers can center their personal conversations with students around the concerns of students. They can refrain from talking about their accomplishments or emphasizing their organizational status. Teachers can employ the same social rules of courtesy with students as are common among adults. They can voluntarily give of their own personal time to help students with those things students believe are important. In short, teachers can choose to behave like likeable people and in doing so students will tend to develop positive attitudes toward them.

Leadership Direction

As indicated before, teachers can influence the motivations of students to try harder to achieve in school if they can develop positive relationships with students. However, being liked or accepted by students is not enough to motivate them to exert more effort to achieve in school. Teachers must also demonstrate to students that they value what they teach highly and have high expectations for academic performance.

If students like their teachers or at least accept them as the legitimate classroom leaders they are inclined to attempt to do whatever they believe their teachers expect them to do. If well-liked teachers behave in ways indicating they believe the subject matter they teach is important students tend to believe it is important too. If teachers establish high expectations for academic performance students tend to attempt to meet these expectations when they accept their teachers as the appropriate leaders of classroom activities.

Teachers will be likely to be consistently perceived as valuing highly the concepts and skills they teach only if they really believe what they teach is important. If teachers do not believe the skills and concepts they teach are important there is little reason to suspect they will be able to convince students what they teach is important. Many teachers cannot justify to others or even articulate to themselves why they teach some of the information, skills, and concepts taught in their classrooms. Much of the value teachers place on learning is intrinsic. They believe knowledge is important simply for the sake of knowing.

Teachers should not feel unduly embarrassed about not being able to demonstrate the importance of everything they teach. It is perfectly acceptable and normal for teachers to value their subject matter intrinsically. Furthermore, as "significant others" and models for students, teachers who value highly the

35

subject matter they teach can greatly influence the feelings of students about the value of learning even when they are unable to explain why learning the subject matter is important. (However, as explained later, they will be even more effective leaders when they can also demonstrate the utility of the content taught.)

A rationale exists for providing students with information, skills, and concepts for which a direct practical application is not apparent. Two commonly accepted logics form the basis for this rationale. The first is that one cannot use knowledge one does not have and once one has knowledge he or she can choose to use it or not - an option not available to the ignorant. The second is that knowledge is the medium of thought. One cannot think without knowledge and greater knowledge increases the ability to think even when considered in isolation from other information the knowledge may be considered impractical or useless. Only when people have obtained a significant volume of information can they perform the higher levels of thinking involved in the synthesis of knowledge to generate creative solutions. In conjunction, these two logics form a valid rationale for teaching information, skills, and concepts that may be only of intrinsic value to teachers, or students, at the time they are taught.

Teachers can demonstrate to students that they place a high value on the information, skills, and concepts they teach in numerous ways. They can plan thoroughly for each class session. If teachers do a good job of planning for their classes they demonstrate to students that they believe what they are teaching is important. Teachers can use the full amount of time available enthusiastically teaching. When teachers spend five to ten minutes at the beginning of each class period getting ready to teach and five to ten minutes at the end of each class closing out instruction they are demonstrating to students that the subject is not even important enough to spend the allotted time teaching.

There are other more subtle ways of demonstrating the importance teachers place on learning. Teachers can zealously guard against class interruptions of all kinds. They can focus all discussions on the content of instruction and refuse to tolerate activities that distract from the planned content. Teachers can spend their discretionary time reading professional books and journals, attending workshops and conferences, or pursuing advanced degrees in their discipline. Each of these can contribute to students perceiving their teachers as valuing learning highly.

Perhaps of greater importance than demonstrating a high value on learning is that teachers hold high expectations for academic performance. Teacher expectations can be viewed in two ways. First, if teachers believe students will perform at high levels their behavior toward students will influence students to perform at higher levels. This may be called a self-fulfilling prophesy. Teachers who believe their students are capable of high levels of performance tend to give feedback to students which fosters positive self-concepts of ability and to establish high standards for performance because they believe their students are capable of meeting high standards. Thus, believing students are capable can influence student effort through both self-concept of ability and teacher-established standards for performance. Of these two, teacher-established standards for performance is perhaps the easiest variable for individual teachers to manipulate to influence the effort students exert to achieve in school.

It is the exceptional, rather than the average, student who does not attempt to meet the minimum standards set by the teacher. Only when the performance standards are believed to be too difficult will the average student not attempt to meet the expectations of teachers they like. If teachers expect little, students tend to give little. When teachers set reasonably high standards for academic performance most students work toward meeting those standards.

Although standardized tests are fixed measures of academic performance with variable scores; i.e. grade equivalents, percentiles, etc.; teachers set the standards for daily performance within their classrooms. The standards established by teachers have a great influence on the effort students exert to learn and learning in turn affects the ability of students to get high scores on standardized tests. Establishing high standards for academic performance within the classroom does not mean giving difficult tests and low grades. Setting high standards means demanding preciseness and accepting no less than accuracy. It means stretching students toward their maximum rates of learning. Setting high expectations for academic performance means maintaining a challenging pace for all students and accepting little less than their best efforts.

INTERNALIZING LOCUS OF CONTROL

When students believe they have a dominant influence on the degree of success they have in school and perceive that success in life is contingent upon success in school they have developed an internal, as opposed to external, locus of control over success in life. Until this internalized locus of control exists, students have little reason for trying to be successful in school.

Each individual pays more attention to and attaches more importance to those aspects of the environment they believe have relevance to their personal welfare. If perceived as having no relevancy to his personal life stimuli from the environment tend to be perceived as unimportant and are largely ignored. If students are to be expected to exert a great deal of effort to achieve in school then they should be aware that what they learn in school will have a direct influence on their personal lives. If they believe otherwise we can expect them to see little utility in achieving in school. Students must learn that they control, to a large extent, their personal futures and what they do in school will have a significant impact on the quality of their lives.

Schooling and Life

Schooling credentials are prerequisites for employment in a wide range of occupations. If for no other reason than this, students should be informed of the employment limitations imposed by the absence of the high school diploma and encouraged to exert the effort necessary to obtain the high school diploma. Without the high school diploma the occupational choices available to young adults are severely limited. For the most part adults without the diploma find they are forced to choose among those occupations where manual labor is at a premium and intellectual skills relatively unimportant. Those who prefer to use their minds more than their bodies will attach more importance to securing a high school diploma when they realize that the diploma is the ticket to being considered for many jobs.

However, for students to be able to hold jobs requiring intellectual skills they must be able to demonstrate those skills. Simply having a high school diploma will not be enough. The employee must have the ability to meet the intellectual requirements of the job or they will not be likely to hold the job. When students realize that the skills they are learning in school will enable them to have the ability to hold the kinds of jobs they prefer they will be more likely to believe the learning opportunities provided in school will affect their economic success in life.

Economic success is only one aspect of quality living. Schooling helps to improve the quality of life in many ways. Schooling helps students to develop the ability to understand interfacing roles in society and to successfully operate within the constraints imposed by society. The information and skills learned in school help individuals to maintain their mental and physical health. Through experiences provided in schools students learn to appreciate and participate in the cultural expressions of the arts and humanities. The potential contributions of schooling to living meaningful and productive lives are limitless. The charge to educators is to communicate and demonstrate to students the importance of schooling to living.

Perhaps, the single most important motivational task of teachers is to demonstrate contingent relationships between what they are teaching and the lives of students outside of the school setting. If they are unable to do this teachers must rely on their human relations skills and the inclinations of students to do those things their teachers expect them to do. Demonstrating contingent relations between schooling experiences and success in life outside school is not an easy task. Much of what is taught in school has little apparent direct utility in life outside of school in the eyes of students. In terms of teaching effectiveness, communication of the reasons for learning specific concepts and skills is equally as important as the methods used in teaching.

Students who see practical applications of mathematics concepts are more likely to try to learn the concepts. When language arts skills are presented in settings that parallel or duplicate situations outside of school students tend to see greater relevance in the skills being taught. Social studies take on a new meaning for students when discussions focus on contemporary concerns. The study of the role

of science in improving the quality of life is
perceived to be more relevant than abstract concepts
presented in isolation from life outside of school.
The specific strategies for demonstrating that what
students learn in school will influence their future
lives will vary from teacher to teacher and from
discipline to discipline. However, an examination of
the unique contributions of the major academic
disciplines provides clues that will be useful in
determining appropriate strategies for these
disciplines.

Academic Relevancy

Language is the medium of verbal communication.
Those who do not have adequate communication skills
cannot let others know their needs or desires. They
are also severely limited in the extent they can make
use of the communications of others. Students
frequently take the adequacy of their vocabulary and
communication skills for granted. Only when they come
face to face with inadequacies in their communications
do they realize they are not effective communicators.
Effective language arts teachers create opportunities
for students to be confronted with and overcome
personal inadequacies in communication skills. These
learning experiences will have greater relevance for
students when the verbal communications focus on topics
of personal interest to them. One of the more
effective means of insuring student interest in topics
of communication is to provide opportunities for them
to choose what they are to talk, write, or read about.

The study of mathematics provides students with
the ability to manipulate abstractions of quantities in
order to solve concrete problems. As their
mathematical skills increase the potential benefits
increase in geometric proportions. Skills limited to
the manipulation of whole numbers are simply inadequate
except for the most rudimentary of applications outside
of the school setting. Computational skills in
manipulations of common fractions, decimals, ratios and
proportions, and algebraic expressions provide students
with the foundations for dealing with the more complex
of problems in life requiring quantitative solutions.
Effective teachers use illustrations that capitalize on
the interests and activities of students in their
personal lives. They help students to cope with "real

41

life" quantitative problems by demonstrating how mathematics skills can provide solutions. Effective teachers use examples of tasks faced by most people in which skill in the manipulation of numbers enables them to effectively complete their tasks. In other words, effective teachers of mathematics bring as much of the outside world into the classroom as frequently as possible.

Science is the discipline that probably has the greatest direct impact on the quality and quantity of life. Students who have an inadequate understanding of scientific principles and do not have the ability to apply these principles not only limit the quality of their lives, but may also directly contribute to a reduction in the length of time they live. The interest of students in the changes that are occuring in their bodies offers a natural focus for the teaching of science. Most students show an interest in the size and shape of their bodies relative to the bodies of their peers. Minor differences are often cause for great concern. Although less conspicious, students are also very interested in the ways their bodies function. Observation of the activities and topics of conversation of students in informal settings will yield additional clues as to ways the teaching of science can be made more relevant to the interests and concerns of students. Only when science is taught in such a manner as to capitalize on the aspects of their personal lives students consider relevant will students perceive the study of science to have high utility.

The study of the social sciences focuses on the social mechanisms of man to adapt to the environment and to provide order to the interactions among individuals and groups within societies. Without knowledge of how these social mechanisms operate, students will invariably be faced with social conflicts throughout their lives. They will not only be ignorant of the rules of behavior, but will have no basis other than their own personal experiences on which to develop principles to guide their social behavior. When students undertake the formal study of the social sciences they can make sense out of the patterns of behavior and determine behaviors that are likely to be condoned or sanctioned. In the early years the social experiences of children are limited primarily to those within the family and to short-term interactions with individuals outside of the family groups. As they grow older students are initiated into more permanent roles within groups.

Effective teachers of the social sciences adapt their instruction to take advantage of the contemporary social concerns of students. If students are taught content enabling them to cope with their contemporary social problems they will perceive social science as having utility. If they are taught how to avoid common social conflicts, they will be more likely to see the study of the social sciences as having relevancy than if the study of social science is presented from a purely historical or authoritarian perspective. In order for social science to be seen as highly useful by students it should be presented in such a way as to be directly related to social problems that confront students or those they believe they will face.

Academic relevance is always judged from an individual perspective. Teachers judge relevance from their point of view and students determine relevance from their perspectives. In terms of improved academic performance, the more critical of the different perspectives is the students' judgments of the relevance of academic experiences. Teachers may perceive subject matter as relevant, but if students do not believe the content to have utility for them they will have little reason to learn it. Although the task may not be easy, all academic courses of study can be taught in such a way as to have relevance for students.

If students do not believe academic performance will benefit them personally, their self-concepts of ability to achieve academically will be relatively unimportant. However, if academic performance is seen as having high utility, then self-concept of ability becomes a critical factor.

Developing Positive Self-Concepts

Self-concepts are developed through an individual's interpretation of feedback received from the environment. Although each person's interpretation is unique, generalizations about the effects of different kinds of stimuli may be made. Positive feedback tends to foster positive self-concepts. Negative feedback generally results in lower

43

self-esteem. The feedback children receive prior to entering school has a large influence on the way they feel about themselves. However, these feelings of self-worth and personal competence are modified throughout life.

Historically, the self-concepts of children become more negative as they receive increasing amounts of negative feedback in schools. Third grade students tend to have more negative self-concepts then first graders and seventh graders have more negative self-concepts than third graders. The same trend continues throughout the schooling years, at least until graduation from secondary schools. This trend can and must be altered if substantial improvements in academic achievement are to become a reality.

For the purposes of the discussion here, self-concepts of ability are of greater concern than general self-esteem or self-concept. The self-concepts of ability that students have in relation to academic performance are developed largely through schooling experiences rather than from experiences outside of the school. (Children are not likely to develop self-concepts of ability to successfully compute the square root of a six-digit number through their experiences outside of the school.) The academic self-concepts of ability of students are largely the direct result of their successes and failures in schools.

When the mode of instruction is based on taping the competitive "instinct" of children (whatever that is) the direct result is often that the self-concepts of ability of most of the unsuccessful students are lowered. In the traditional form of competition among students within classrooms there are few winners and the only people whose self-concepts of ability are likely to be improved through competition are the winners. Negative consequences are the most likely results for the self-concepts of ability of the losers. Classroom practices that result in the devlopment of more positive self-concepts of ability for all students should be based upon the principle that each student should have significantly more successes than failures within the classroom.

Teachers can develop instructional techniques for improving the self-concepts of ability of their

44

students. However, many will find themselves with intense internal conflicts. They will find it difficult to give positive feedback for performance they feel is inadequate for the grade level or subject matter they are teaching. The feeling that they must maintain academic standards will be so strong they cannot permit themselves to instruct students at the students' levels of cognitive development. But, they really have no viable alternative if fostering positive self-concepts are desired. Students cannot reliably be successful unless they have learned the foundational information, skills, and concepts enabling them to progress through the curriculum. As long as students are placed in instructional settings where they cannot be successful the effects on self-concepts of ability can only be negative.

Effective instructional strategies used by teachers to foster positive self-concepts of ability begin with the appropriate placement of students into the curricular structure. Students must be taught at levels where they can be successful and teachers should constantly seek opportunities to give positive feedback that is perceived as legitimate. The process is arduous, but well worth the effort.

Several general guidelines will prove useful in designing strategies to improve the self-concepts of ability of students. Praise whenever possible. Avoid criticism whenever possible. Never withhold feelings of acceptance from the child simply because of unacceptable behavior. Disapprove of the behavior if necessary, but never disapprove of the individual. Nearly all people feel better about themselves following praise they perceive as legitimate. Negative feedback will most often have either negative or neutral consequences. If perceived as legitimate it lowers self-concept. If perceived as nonlegitimate it may have no effect on self-concept, but probably will affect the student's perception of the legitimacy of future feedback. Disapproval of students because of their behavior tends to render the teacher impotent as a social influence on self-concepts of ability. An unaccepting attitude on the part of teachers toward students causes teachers to become "nonsignificant others" to most students.

Teachers who trust students and give them responsibility are contributing to the development of

positive self-concepts of ability. When teachers
demonstrate to students that they trust them they are
telling students "I trust you because I know you can do
it." An added advantage of this philosophical position
is that students tend to be reluctant to betray that
trust and work harder to ensure their success thereby
increasing the liklihood they will be successful which
leads to a more positive self-concept of ability. An
attitude of distrust contributes to self-doubt and
lowered self-concepts of ability.

DEVELOPING INTEGRATED PLANS*

Serious attempts to raise academic performance to optimal levels should take into consideration activities to structure learning experiences, using external resources, developing positive attitudes toward teachers, demonstrating high expectations for academic performance, developing positive self-concepts of ability, and demonstrating the future utility of schooling. This, obviously, is no easy task. However, because of the complex interactions among the six variable factors, each must be adequately addressed or beneficial effects in one area may be offset by negative consequences in another area. The most promising plans integrate activities in all six areas into one comprehensive plan. This can best be accomplished by approaching the task through a clearly defined set of unique activities.

Goal Setting

As discussed in the section on methods of structuring learning experiences, the first activity is that of clearly defining the learning outcomes desired and determining how these outcomes are to be measured. Until this process is completed the best that can be hoped for is that because of improvements in motivation and the use of better resources general increases in learning may be reflected in changes in whatever instruments may be used to measure learning outcomes.

The process of defining the learning outcomes desired identifies the terminal goal of all other activities. The efficient and effective use of external resources can contribute to the accomplishment of these previously identified learning outcomes. Motivation of students can be directed toward getting students to exert more effort toward attaining the skills and concepts necessary to improve their test

---

*   Portions of this chapter were taken from: Kenneth M. Matthews and C. Thomas Holmes, "Improving Test Scores - How to Develop Comprehensive Plans," **The NASSP Bulletin**, Vol. 67, No. 460 (February, 1983), pp. 104-112.

scores. Ability, effort, and the use of resources without direction are, at best, inefficient and, at worst, counter-productive. Once the learning outcomes are defined then the important task of assessing needs can be undertaken.

Needs may be defined as discrepancies between desired and existing conditions. The desired motivational states of students are considered to be: 1) Positive attitudes toward teachers. 2) Perceptions of teachers holding moderately high expectations for and values of academic academic performance. 3) Belief that success in life is enhanced through success in school, and 4) Moderately positive self-concepts of ability to achieve in school. Before initiating strategies to create these conditions, assessment of existing motivational states would be highly desirable for two reasons. First generating generalized strategies to have a positive effect on all four variables at the same time is extremely difficult. Second, trying to raise the state of motivation in a variable that is already at an optimal level may have negative effects on effort.

Most teachers do a reasonably good job of motivating most students most of the time. But sometimes one or more of the four variables are neglected and undesirable motivational states allowed to develop. If for no other reason than to insure that individual motivational variables are not overlooked, the status of all four motivational variables should be assessed.

Collecting Data

In order for assessment techniques to be used effectively certain conditions must be met. The technique must require relatively little time to execute and interpret. Teaching is simply too important to spend an inordinate amount of time diagnosing motivational states. Educators are well-advised to devote the vast majority of their energy to generating strategies to motivate students or to improve methods of improving instruction. No matter how potentially useful, if assessment of student motivation takes too much time away from direct instruction resistance should be expected and avoided.

If the results of the assessment techniques are to be meaningful they must be credible. Personal judgments by educators without other supporting data are rarely an acceptable method of assessing student motivation. Diagnosed motivational needs are much more likely to be accepted if they are in quantifiable terms and are generated through objective means. Although the perceptions and judgments of students can seldom be taken at face value, they are preferable to the judgments of educators, particularly if they are given in response to standardized stimuli under nonthreatening conditions. Student perceptions and judgments tempered by the opinions of teachers and other educators are even more desirable. It seems likely that brief questionnaires, completed by students under standardized nonthreatening conditions, coupled with the judgments of teachers and other educators, is the most acceptable means of producing data for assessment of the motivational status of students. However, the contents of the questionnaire must be carefully selected if meaningful data are to be generated.

In assessing students' attitudes toward teachers the questions should focus directly on the inclinations of students to follow their teachers' leadership. Questions related to students' perceptions of their teachers' expectations and values should be designed to give indications of the extent teachers really want and demand excellence in their academic work. Questions referring to students' perceptions of the future utility of academic performance should be multidimensional so as to encompass the major dimensions of life outside of school considered to be important by students. In assessing the self-concepts of ability of students the questions should be designed to indicate the perceptions of students of the probability they can be academically successful. An additional consideration in the design of questionnaires for assessing student motivation is that of generating information which provides clues as to strategies which may be effective in overcoming motivational deficiencies. Although other instruments may be appropriate and useful, a copy of a questionnaire specifically designed to meet these criteria is included in the Appendix.[58]

Interpreting Data

Instruments such as the **Student Achievement Diagnostic Questionnaire** (see Appendix) provide data, in numerical form, for assessing each of the four critical motivational variables. Once quantifiable measures are available several options can be considered. Normative data for individual schools or classes can be produced and strategies can be developed to work on the motivational variable with the greatest deficiency or specific variables can be selected as the targets of improvement strategies based upon the judgments of those who have intimate knowledge of the students under consideration.

Using the results of assessment data to make judgments as to which variables would most likely be critical to the improvement of effort of the students involved requires considerable insight into the orientations and motivations of these students. For example, if the students clearly plan to seek employment after graduation from high school, then their responses to questions such as "How much will school help you in your future work?" and "How much will school help you to be successful?" should be examined closely. On the other hand, if teachers have a history of issuing a high percentage of failing grades, then their responses to the question "How good are you at getting high scores in school?" can provide useful insight into the impact of grading practices of students' self-concepts of ability.

For most groups, teachers' expectations for academic performance have the greatest impact on the effort students exert to achieve. The motivational variable considered second in impact is students' perceptions of the future utility of academic performace. Third in importance is self-concept of ability to achieve in school. Of least importance of the four motivational factors seems to be that of the students' attitudes toward their teachers. With this generalization as a guide, the ranking of the numerical response of students should be:

> First - Teacher expectations
> Second - Future utility
> Third - Self-concept of ability
> Fourth - Attitude toward teachers

If the responses of the students are not in this order, then the primary target variable would be the highest priority variable which is out of order. For example, if scores for Future Utility are lower than the Self-Concept of Ability and Attitude Toward Teachers' scores then students' perceptions of the Future Utility of achieving in school should be the primary target variable. On the other hand, if the responses of students are in the desire order, then Teachers' Expectations may be the appropriate primary target variable. Other techniques may appropriately be used and the relative impact of the four motivational variables will vary from student to student. However, this technique will provide teachers with a useful way of selecting motivational variables on which to focus their strategies to improve the motivations of groups of students to achieve in school.

Selecting Strategies

Because of highly complex interactive effects of strategies to improve student motivation the process of selecting strategies should be undertaken with considerable caution. It is obvious that if teachers expectations are set at such a high level that only a few students ever pass their tests, then students should have relatively low concepts of their ability to pass those tests. Other interactions are more subtle.

Some strategies are perfectly logical for improvement in one motivational variable yet have strong negative effects on another motivational variable. For example, teachers may focus their classroom illustrations and discussions on the more common concerns of students in their lives outside of school to improve students' perceptions of the utility of achieving in school. But if the academic performance measure deals primarily with conceptual skills such as the ability to synthesize information for the generation of solutions of abstract problems, then students are likely to perceive their teachers as valuing the solutions to abstract problems less than if more of the classroom activities dealt with problems which focused on the development of conceptual skills. Although there need be no conflicting effects, unless strategies are cautiously selected such consequences may be expected.

51

Absolute certainty that negative effects will not result from implemented strategies to improve student motivation will never exist. However, there are procedures that will produce effective strategies which will have few, if any, negative effects. A recommended procedure for selecting motivational strategies involves three simple steps. First, identify and rank in terms of anticipated effectiveness as many ways of improving the target motivational factor as possible without taking into consideration any possible effects on other factors. Second, rate the probable positive effects of each technique generated in step one on each of the other motivational factors. Third, select those techniques which would most likely be effective in improving the target variable and, at the same time, would not result in negative effects on other motivational factors.

Questions teachers may find helpful in generating and selecting strategies to improve student motivation are:

1. Are you friendly, helpful, and cheerful?

2. Are you consistent and predictable in your interactions with students?

3. Do students believe you care about them as individuals?

4. Do you treat students as social equals?

5. Do you spend your discretionary time helping students with "their" problems?

6. Do you believe what you are teaching is highly important?

7. Do you plan for each minute of the allotted instructional time?

8. Are you enthusiastic about what you are teaching?

9. Do you demonstrate intolerance with distractions from the teaching-learning process?

10. Do you demand preciseness and no less than accuracy in your students' work?

11. Do you set a challenging pace for students and accept little less their best efforts?

12. Are students taught at a level where they experience many more successes than failures?

13. Does each student in your classes receive positive feedback from you each day?

14. Do your students believe you trust them and have confidence in their ability?

15. Do you refrain from criticizing students?

16. Do you believe your students are capable of higher levels of academic performance.

17. Do you emphasize job-related applications of content you teach?

18. Do you use situations that occur outside of school in your illustrations and discussions?

19. Do you focus more on the present and future than on the past in your classroom activities?

20. Do you try to use the concerns of students as a vehicle for teaching?

Once strategies for improving student motivation have been selected they can be integrated with strategies for structuring learning experiences and using external resources into a plan for improving academic performance.

Integrated Plans

Systematic integration of the various components of plans to improve student achievement is not extremely complicated, but is a valuable process to ensure that none of the components are neglected. The list below identified events that should occur in the process of implementing and evaluating integrated plans. Relations among these events are shown in Figure 3.

A. Learning outcome goals are identified.

B. Methods and instruments for assessing learning outcomes are identified.

C. Methods and instruments for assessing student motivation are identified.

D. Motivational states are assessed.

E. Student abilities are assessed.

F. Deficiencies in student abilities are identified.

G. Deficiencies in student motivation are identified.

H. Structures for learning experiences are identified.

I. Strategies for improving student motivation are identified.

J. Potential conflicts between strucutures for learning experiences and strategies for improving student motivation are identified and resolved.

K. External resources are identified and available.

L. Strategies for improving academic performance are implemented.

M. Progress is assessed.

As Figure 3 illustrates, the relationship between ability and effort are such that one cannot be effectively considered in isolation from the other. Furthermore, strategies for the efficient use of external resources cannot be effectively implemented until abilities and motivations are assessed. The point is that planning for academic improvement is a continuous and interactive process. However, by following the steps identified in Figure 3 the process can be made more orderly

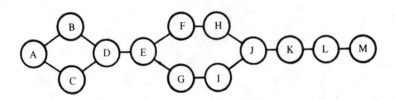

Figure 3 - Integrated Plans

SUMMARY

This publication presents a conceptual model for improving academic performance, describes techniques for structuring learning experiences, using human and material resources, providing effective leadership, developing internalized locus of control in students, and explains how each of the component parts of planning can be integrated and coordinated. Academic performance is described as being directly affected by the three key variables of ability, effort, and external resources. Ability and effort are, in turn, considered to be influenced by other factors.

Ability is described as the product of the interaction between inherited capacity to learn and learning experiences. Because inherited capacity to benefit from experience is beyond the influence of schooling, educators are advised to concentrate on providing appropriate learning experiences in order to develop the ability of students to get high test scores. Appropriate learning experiences are described as those that provide students with the ability to perform, and, at the same time, insure that resources are not allocated toward increasing ability when greater ability is not needed to perform at acceptable levels.

Effort is described as being directly influenced by students' self-concepts of ability to achieve and their desires to achieve. Those students who perceive they have little possibility of being successful in school can reasonably be expected to exert little effort to achieve in school. Students who do not want to achieve can be expected to do little to achieve. However, three factors affected by schooling experiences are presented as appropriate targets for strategies to motivate students to achieve in school. Attitudes toward teachers, perceptions of teachers' expectations and values of academic performance, and perceptions of the future utility of academic performance are described as having a strong influence on the desire of students to achieve academically.

The relationships between factors affecting effort and performance are described as being nonlinear. Too positive a self-concept of ability may lead to less, rather than greater effort to achieve. Too high a level of desire may lead to disabling anxiety.

Moderately positive self-concepts of ability and moderately strong desires to learn are preferred motivational states.

Ability, effort, and external resources each influence academic performance, but the interactions among the three factors are more important considerations. Performance cannot occur without a threshold level of ability, sufficient effort, and adequate resources. Because of this and the potential for differential effects of specific acts caution against the use of simplistic approaches is advised.

Appropriate structures for learning experiences are described as those which are logical in nature. That is, those in which basic information is mastered before students are expected to apply cognitive processing strategies using the basic information. Logical structures include those in which foundational skills and concepts are taught first. Appropriate structures for learning experiences begin with diagnosis of the deficiencies that exist in the current abilities of students and then proceed with prescriptive instruction based on these deficiencies. Prescriptions consist of teaching students those precise skills and concepts that are necessary for acceptable levels of academic performance. Instead of expecting students to develop individual-specific cognitive strategies independently, educators are advised to teach students cognitive strategies which can be applied and providing them with opportunities to use these strategies.

The key to the effective use of external resources is the extent the resources focus on the skills and concepts measured. Textbooks and other material resources can be used most effectively when the content is congruent with test content. Human resources are most productive when they assist students in learning the skills and concepts that are measured.

The influence of instructional leadership on the desire of students to achieve in school is expressed through positive teacher-student relations and students believing their teachers have moderately high expectations. Students who like their teachers exert more effort to please their teachers. If they also believe their teachers expect them to learn they try harder to learn what their teachers are attempting to teach.

When students believe what is taught in school will be useful to them outside of the school setting they will be motivated to learn what their teachers are attempting to teach. Teachers who stress applications of skills and concepts to life outside of school increase the likelihood students will see utility in learning the skills and concepts being taught in school.

The development of integrated plans for improving academic performances is critical if consistency in results can be anticipated. Although extremely complex interactions can occur among the six variable factors, the process of developing integrated plans can be made more orderly by:

1. Clearly specifying the learning outcomes desired.

2. Identifying both the methods and instruments for asessing academic performance before attempting to teach.

3. Assessing motivational states of students prior to treatment.

4. Assessing the abilities of individual students prior to treatment.

5. Designing strategies to correct identified deficiencies in student motivation.

6. Struturing learning experiences for students which build upon existing abilities.

7. Resolving potential conflicts between component parts of plans before implementation.

This monograph provides the foundation for comprehensive and realistic approaches to improve student achievement. It contains both elements of successful programs -- a sound theoretical base and practical methods.

REFERENCE NOTES

[1] For example see: Robert F. Alioto and J. A. Jungherr, **Operational PPBS for Education** (New York: Harper and Row, 1971); Margaret B. Carpenter and Sue A. Haggart, "Cost Effectiveness Analysis for Educational Planning," **Educational Technology** 10(1970): 26-30; William H. Curtis, ed., **Educational Resource Management System** (Chicago: Research Corporation of the Association of School Business Officials, 1971); Roy H. Forbes, "Cost Effectiveness Analysis: Primer and Guidelines," **Program Budgeting for School District Planning** (Englewood Cliffs, N.J.: The Rand Corporation, 1972); and Stephen J. Knezevich, **Program Budgeting -- (PPBS)** (Berkeley, CA: McCutchan Publishing Corporation, 1973).

[2] Among the better known are: Harvey A. Averch et al., **How Effective is Schooling? A Critical Review of Research** (Englewood Cliffs, NJ: Educational Technology Publications, 1974); James S. Coleman et al., **Equality of Educational Opportunity** (Washington, DC: U.S. Government Printing Office, 1966); and Christopher Jencks et al., **Inequality -- A Reassessment of the Effect of Family and Schooling in America** (New York: Basic Books, 1972).

[3] John I. Goodlad, "A Perspective on Accountability," **Phi Delta Kappan** 57(1975): 108-112.

[4] Averch et al., **Effective**, p. 171.

[5] John W. Atkinson, "The Mainsprings of Achievement-Oriented Activity," in **Motivation and Achievement**, ed. John W. Atkinson and Joel O. Raynor (Washington, DC: H. V. Winston and Sons, 1974), p. 37.

[6] A discussion of considerations in selecting conceptual tools is presented by Kenneth D. Benne, Robert Chin, and Warren G. Bennis in "Science and Practice," **The Planning of Change**, 3rd ed., ed. Warren G. Bennis, Kenneth D. Benne, Robert Chin, and Kenneth E. Corey (New York: Holt, Rinehart, and Winston, 1976), pp. 28-37.

[7] This model expands upon basic concepts and models reported earlier. See: Kenneth M. Matthews and Carvin L. Brown, "Schooling and Learning -- The

Principal's Influence on Student Achievement," **The NASSP Bulletin** 60(October 1976): 1-15.

[8] David E. Lavin, **The Prediction of Academic Performance** (New York: The Russel Sage Foundation, 1965), p. 43.

[9] David C. McClelland et al., **Talent and Society: New Perspectives in the Identification of Talent** (New York: D. Van Nostrand Co., 1958), p. 13.

[10] Wilbur B. Brookover and Edsel L. Erickson, **Sociology of Education** (Homewood, IL: The Dorsey Press, 1975), p. 265.

[11] Robert M. Gagne', **The Conditions of Learning** (New York: Holt, Rinehart, and Winston, 1965), p. 25.

[12] Averch et al., **Effective**, p. 167.

[13] John L. Spaeth, "Cognitive Comlexity: A Dimension Underlying the Socioeconomic Achievement Process," in **Schooling and Achievement in American Society**, ed. William H. Sewell, Robert M. Houser, and David J. Featherman (New York: Academic Press, 1976), p. 119. This point is supported by the findings reported by Scott Thomson and Nancy DeLeonibus in **Guidelines for Improving SAT Scores** (Reston, VA: National Association of Secondary School Principals, 1978), p. 5.

[14] Patricia C. Smith and C. J. Cranny, "Psychology of Men at Work," **Annual Review of Psychology** 19(1968): 469.

[15] Averch et al., **Effective**, p. 65.

[16] Victor H. Vroom, **Work and Motivation** (New York: John Wiley and Sons, 1964).

[17] Ibid., p. 18.

[18] Atkinson, "Mainsprings," p. 13.

[19] Coleman et al., **Equality**, pp. 319-321.

[20] William W. Purkey, "The Self and Academic Achievement," **Research Bulletin of the Florida**

Educational Research and Development Council, Spring 1967.

[21] William B. Brookover, Edsel L. Erickson, and L. M. Joiner, **Self-Concept of Ability and School Achievement: Relation of Self-Concept to Achievement in High School** (East Lansing, MI: Michigan State University and United States Office of Education Cooperative Research Project No. 2831, 1967), pp. 145-146.

[22] Richard J. Shavelson, Judith H. Hubner, and George C. Stanton, "Self-Concept: Validation of Construct Interpretations," **Review of Educatioal Research** 46(Summer 1976), p. 436.

[23] Brookover and Erickson, **Sociology,** p. 280.

[24] Atkinson, "Mainspring," p. 34.

[25] Ibid., p. 17.

[26] John W. Atkinson, "Strength of Motivation and Efficiency of Performance," in **Motivation and Achievement**, ed. J. W. Atkinson and J. O. Raynor (Washington, DC: H. V. Winston and Sons, 1974), p. 201.

[27] David C. McClelland, **The Achieving Society** (Princeton, NJ: D. Van Nostrand Company, 1961) and D. C. McClelland, **Personality** (New York: The Dryden Press, 1951).

[28] Averch et al., **Effective,** p. 51.

[29] Edmond H. Weiss, "The Missing Variable in Input - Output Studies," **Planning and Changing** 4(Winter 1974), pp. 203-210.

[30] "Schools Do Make a Difference," **Today's Education**, November-December 1975, pp. 24-31.

[31] Carvin L. Brown, "Identification of Fiscal Characteristics Associated with Local School District Productivity in Georgia," (Ed.D. dissertation, University of Florida, 1974).

[32] William B. Castetter, **The Personnel Function in Educational Administration**, 2nd ed. (New York: Macmillan, 1976), p. 21.

[33] This is the position taken by Stephen J. Knezevich, **Administration of Public Education** (New York: Harper and Row, 1969), p. 14.

[34] Amitai Etzioni, **A Comparative Analysis of Complex Organizations** (New York: The Free Press, 1961).

[35] James M. Lipham and James A. Hoeh, Jr., **The Principalship: Foundations and Functions** (New York: Harper and Row, 1974), p. 94.

[36] Ralph B. Kimbrough and Michael Y. Nunnery, **Educational Administration -- An Introduction** (New York: Macmillan, 1976), p. 146.

[37] Douglas McGregor, **Leadership and Motivation** (Cambridge, MA: The MIT Press, 1966).

[38] Knezevich, **Administration of Public Education**, pp. 144-146.

[39] Robert B. Blake and Jane S. Mouton, **The Managerial Grid** (Houston: Gulf, 1964).

[40] Frederick W. Hertzberg, "Motivation Through Job Enrichment," in **Motivation and Productivity**, ed. S. S. Gellerman (Washington, DC: BNA Inc., 1967) (Film Series).

[41] Fred E. Fiedler, **Theory of Leadership Effectiveness** (New York: McGraw-Hill, 1967).

[42] Knezevich, **Administration of Public Education**, pp. 15-16.

[43] For a discussion of the importance of attitudes on behavior see: Milton Rokeach, **Attitudes and Values, Theory of Organization and Change** (San Francisco: Jossey Bass, 1968) and "The Nature of Attitudes," in **International Encyclopedia of the Social Sciences**, 1968.

[44] Rensis Likert, "The Management of Human Assets" in **Motivation and Productivity**, ed. S. S. Gellerman (Washington, DC: BNA Inc., 1967) (Film Series).

[45] The influence of social background on individual behavior within groups has been well-documented. Two of the better known reports are: James S. Coleman,

The Adolescent Society (New York, The Free Press of Glencoe, 1961) and August B. Hollingshead, Elmtown's Youth, The Impact of Social Classes on Adolescents (New York: John Wiley and Sons, 1949).

[46] The foundation for this position rests on the analysis of group behavior provided by George C. Homans, The Human Group (New York: Harcourt, Brace, and World, 1950).

[47] Edward L. McDill, Leo C. Rigsby, and Edmund D. Meyers, Jr., "Educational Climates of High Schools: Their Effects and Sources," The American Journal of Sociology, ERIC ED 004500 and Edward L. McDill, Edward D. Meyers, Jr., and Leo C. Rigsby, "Institutional Effects of Academic Behavior of High School Students," Sociology of Education 40(1967), pp. 181-199.

[48] This relationship is implied from Rokeach's definition of attitudes, See: Rokeach, Attitudes, p. 450.

[49] Jonathan L. Freeman, J. Merrill Carlsmith, and David O. Sears, Social Psychology (Englewood Cliffs, NJ: Prentice-Hall, 1970), p.371.

[50] Vroom, Work, p. 219.

[51] Averch et al., Effective, p. 64. Expectations may be considered only one possible indication of the value a superior has on performance. However, it appears to be the major factor considered in the literature.

[52] Brookover and Erickson, Sociology, pp. 315-316.

[53] Averch et al., Effective, p. 65.

[54] John W. Atkinson, Willy Lens, and P. M. O'Malley, "Motivation and Ability: Interactive Psychological Determinants of Intellective Performance, Educational Achievement, and Each Other" in Schooling and Achievement in American Society, ed. Robert M. Hauser and David J. Featherman (New York: Academic Press, 1976), p. 38.

[55] McDill et al., "Educational Climates" and "Institutional Effects."

[56] "I" has been deleted from the expression because schooling experiences have no effect on the inherited capacity of students to benefit from experience.

[57] Kenneth M. Matthews, "Improving Academic Performance," **Educational Forum** XLIV(November 1979), p. 66.

[58] A longer version of this instrument is described in: Kenneth M. Matthews and Tak Chung Chan, "Referent Differences in Pupil Motivation," **Educational and Psychological Measurement** 42(Summer 1980), pp. 531 -536.

APPENDIX

STUDENT ACHIEVEMENT DIAGNOSTIC QUESTIONNAIRE
(short form)

1. How much do your teachers want you to learn?

   Strong ⑦ ⑥ ⑤ ④ ③ ② ① Weak

2. How much do you want to do what your teachers like you to do?

   Strong ⑦ ⑥ ⑤ ④ ③ ② ① Weak

3. How much do your teachers want you to study?

   Large ⑦ ⑥ ⑤ ④ ③ ② ① Small

4. How much will school help you in your future work?

   Small ① ② ③ ④ ⑤ ⑥ ⑦ Large

5. How much do you like to please your teachers?

   Low ① ② ③ ④ ⑤ ⑥ ⑦ High

6. How much will school help you to be successful?

   Small ① ② ③ ④ ⑤ ⑥ ⑦ Large

7. How important do your teachers think school is?

   Low ① ② ③ ④ ⑤ ⑥ ⑦ High

8. How much do your teachers please you?

   Low ① ② ③ ④ ⑤ ⑥ ⑦ High

9. How much will school help you to do what you want to do in life?

   Large ⑦ ⑥ ⑤ ④ ③ ② ① Small

10. How much do your teachers want you to do your best?

    Low ① ② ③ ④ ⑤ ⑥ ⑦ High

11. How good are you at getting high scores in school?

    High ⑦ ⑥ ⑤ ④ ③ ② ① Low

12. How much will school help you to live a better life?

    Large ⑦ ⑥ ⑤ ④ ③ ② ① Small

13. How good a student are you in school?

    Bad ① ② ③ ④ ⑤ ⑥ ⑦ Good

14. How much do you like the way your teachers work with you?

    Large ⑦ ⑥ ⑤ ④ ③ ② ① Small

15. What is your true ability in school?

    Low ① ② ③ ④ ⑤ ⑥ ⑦ High

16. How good are you at learning in school?

    Good ⑦ ⑥ ⑤ ④ ③ ② ① Bad

Reprinted from **The NASSP Bulletin**, Vol. 67, No. 460, page 111.